The Ultimate Charismatic Growth

KATE HIXSON

The Ultimate Charismatic Growth

First edition

This book was professionally typeset on Reedsy.

Find out more at reedsy.com

Contents

1

Chapter 1

What is Charisma?

Charismaisthequalityofbeingabletoattract,enchantandinfluence those around you. It is typically easy to detect when someone is charming. It is, however, frequently much harder to say exactly what abilities or attributes those people have that other, less charismatic, people lack.

To make things more confusing, there are many types of charismatic persons.

Some may be quieter, maybe depending more on their personal charm than their words to influence others. Others are enthusiastic communicators, sweeping everyone along with their excitement.

Ultimately, charisma is the outcome of outstanding communication and interpersonal abilities. It is therefore feasible to cultivate and strengthen your charisma.

charisma consists of a mixture of what they called '**affability**' and

'**influence**'.

There are a variety of skills that make up influence and affability. Each of these can be developed, given time and effort 1

THE ULTIMATE CHARISMATIC GROWTH

Developing Influence

The statements used to assess charisma reveal that influence often has three key parts:

-presence,

-ability to influence, and

-ability to lead.

Presence is possibly the most difficult to define and pin down. However, persons with presence can generally be regarded to be confident and believe in themselves, and also be positive and resilient in the face of adversity.

Charismatic people are confident people – or at least have the capacity to appear confident.

Being confident to speak in a range of contexts, one-to-one, in groups and in front of crowds is a talent that many individuals struggle with. A charismatic person can not only appear confident in communicating, but they can also assist others feel confidence too, therefore aiding and strengthening the communication process. Charismatic people are confident in a positive sense, without being boastful or conceited.

As with confidence, charismatic people are, or have the ability to appear, optimistic.

This means they attempt to see the best in other people, situations and occurrences. They usually remain optimistic and bounce back from setbacks, because they have high resilience. Charismatic persons have the power to persuade others to see things as they do, thus they can energize and assist others to feel more positive.

Positive thinking and optimism can be significant forces for successful negotiating and problem-solving.

Charismatic people also have very good persuading and influencing skills.

They can often make people want what they want and unite them in a single goal.

This skill can be utilized for both good and bad. Charismatic leaders may be able to inspire and encourage their people to undertake things that can even appear unachievable. They can motivate people to perform arduous jobs. A charismatic confidence trickster, however, may be able to use their abilities to acquire the trust and respect of their victims before ultimately extorting money or other goods.

The third attribute considered as part of 'influence' is that charismatic people frequently have very high leadership skills.

They may be perceived as 'natural leaders', even though they have typically spent years honing their talents to make leadership seem smooth. They are able to use a number of leadership styles to suit the circumstances, and people whom they are leading. They are also usually very effective at formulating and then presenting a captivating vision; their general communication abilities are often exceptionally great.

Developing Affability

The primary elements of affability include the ability to get on with people, smiling often—and genuinely—and being able to make people feel comfortable. Perhaps the most significant piece of this is high emotional intelligence.

The capacity to appear confident and/or optimistic if you are not involves a certain level of 'acting'. It demands you to be in command of your emotions.

You also need to be able to harness both your own and others' emotions positively to achieve what you want.

Charismatic people are particularly effective at displaying their actual feelings when this works to their greatest benefit. They are usually also skilled at

concealing or acting in a way that makes others believe what they perceive.

The comparison of a swimming swan is applicable in this example, peaceful and serene on the surface but with a lot of concealed activity out of view to the casual observer.

Charismatic people are interesting: others want to listen to what they have

to say.

This is partially because they have intriguing things to say—such as a compelling vision—and partly the way that they communicate.

They are frequently good storytellers, with a captivating approach when speaking and explaining. They are able to deliver their message clearly and simply, being serious and introducing humor where needed to keep their audience attention and focused. When they are in one-on-one or small group scenarios, charismatic people will utilize open, relaxed, body language involving lots of eye contact. They will watch for reaction from their audience and explain their position accordingly. When in larger groups or making a presentation to others, body language will be more exaggerated in an attempt to incorporate everybody.

Charismatic people are also interested: they genuinely want to listen to

what others have to say.

They are likely to ask open questions to help them understand the thoughts, ideas and feelings of others and, because of their ability to make others feel at ease, will often get honest and emotional answers. Charismatic people tend to be empathic and considerate towards others, remembering information from earlier conversations and consequently acquiring respect and trust.

Charismatic persons are adept at developing rapport with others.

A true smile, maintaining eye contact, being nice and kind is a very powerful way of getting people on your side. People are far more willing to do things for you if they are treated nicely and you are polite to them.

2

Chapter 2

Why Charismatic Growth

Charismaisintimatelytiedtoassertiveness,whichweallneed,if only for defensive reasons. Charisma is not just about showing off.

Charisma enables us to influence (and inspire) people, and also to change our external environment, which from time to time we all need to do - even the introverts among us. Time management, for example, crucially depends on regulating our environment and the expectations of others.

If you want to grow a business, lead a team, be a teacher or a trainer or a speaker, or maybe enter politics, then you have more reasons for improving your charismatic powers.

Charisma is not an always-on aura that only extraordinary individuals possess. Charisma is a power of human personality which may be understood, measured, and cultivated. And while some people seem more inherently charismatic than others, the truth is that everyone - given belief and work -

can develop charismatic power, either as a conscious activity to be employed when needed, or as a deeper ‘second nature’.

Charisma is useful for inspiring others, leading a team, or teaching and developing individuals, or being an innovator or a fund-raiser.

Charisma is also helpful for project-management, problem-solving, facili-tating and pioneering.

And charisma is of course useful for all sorts of human connections - dating, mating, parenting, etc.

Charisma helps in any situation when you need or desire to influence other people and external elements.

When you see charisma in these terms - and also as a technique of understanding and directing your own strength of character - you might also see reasons in your own life for wanting to acquire some charismatic power for yourself.

The Components of Charisma.

Presence

When you think about charisma, you might think of attempting to make yourself seem incredibly amazing to others. But the paradoxical secret of charisma is that it's not about trumpeting your wonderful traits, but making the other person feel good about himself. Real charisma helps the other person feel significant; when they complete an interaction with you, they feel better about themselves than they did before.

Focusing your mental and emotional energy on someone while you connect is how you create that sensation of importance. People essentially crave attention – they want to be recognized and appreciated.

And you don't have to be an extroverted, uber-social extrovert in order to have and express charisma. There have been plenty of magnetic individuals throughout history who have successfully counterbalanced their introverted inclinations with a charismatically intense focus and presence: Instead of 6 being the life of the party, chatting everybody up, and offering a little of themselves to a lot of people, they concentrate on giving their full attention to a few; in so doing, they make others feel incredibly special. Charisma isn't necessarily about quantity, but quality.

Conveying presence is a simple concept, but oftentimes difficult to actually achieve. You can't just fake it. People are surprisingly competent at deciphering your faux interest. To effectively portray presence, you must actually be present. It takes a tremendous amount of willpower to focus all your attention on the person you're with at the moment. But like everything things, with practice, it becomes substantially easier.

How to Develop Your Charismatic Presence.

Bring yourself to the here and now.

Presence originates in your mind. If you feel like your mind is off somewhere else while connecting with someone, try this simple practice to bring yourself back to the here and now: Focus on physical feelings in your body that you normally disregard. It could be your breath or it could be the sense of your feet contacting the earth. You don't have to spend very long focusing on these experiences. Just a second or two will put you back into the moment you're enjoying with this individual.

Make sure you're physically comfortable.

It's hard to be truly present with someone when all you're thinking about is how painfully tight your clothes are or how hot it is. To that end, do what you can to ensure you're as comfortable as possible. That doesn't necessary mean wearing a sweatsuit; being trendy, and feeling gorgeous, makes you feel much more confidence, and the more confident you feel, the more charismatic you'll come off. But it does require wearing clothing that fit. Wearing well-fitted duds will make you both look and feel better. Other things you can do to boost your physical comfort include getting adequate sleep, laying off the caffeine (be calm instead of jittery), and adjusting the thermostat (when you

can) to a more comfortable temperature.

Set your devices on mute and put them out of sight.

This serves two objectives. First, it limits the temptation for you to check them when you're talking with someone. Second, it sends a strong message to the person you're with that they have your undivided focus and they're not sharing it with the smartphone put on the table.

Look the person in the eye when they're talking.

Numerous studies have indicated that people who make higher degrees of eye contact with others are viewed as exhibiting a lot of positive attributes, including warmth, honesty, sincerity, competency, confidence, and emotional stability. And not only does increasing eye contact make you seem more enticing in pretty much every aspect to individuals you engage with, it also increases the quality of that interaction. Eye contact provides a sense of intimacy to your interactions, and leaves the receiver of your gaze feeling more positive about your interaction and also more connected to you.

Nod to express that you're listening.

Besides eye contact, one simple way to express presence is through body language, and more specifically, nodding your head. But be judicious with the noggin nods. An oversupply can signal you're working too hard to please and agree with the person, which diminishes their view of your strength. Also, only nod at relevant times; you'll need to be actually listening to recognize when a nod makes sense.

Ask Clarifying Question

An easy method to show someone that you're entirely there with them is to offer clarifying questions after he or she has spoken. For example, you could say, "Tell me more about why you feel that way.In more casual interactions, ask people questions such, "What was your favorite part of that?" or "What was the hardest part of that for you?" People genuinely love reflecting on and answering such topics.

Avoid fidgeting.

Fidgeting conveys to the other person that you're not comfortable or content and that there's somewhere else you'd rather be. So don't twiddle your thumbs or your phone. And resist looking around for what else is going 8

on, which communicates to the other person that you're searching for a better opportunity than your current one

Don't think about how you're going to answer while the individual is still talking.

We all have a predisposition to do this. Our inner conversational narcissist wants to be ready to jump in and start chatting as soon as there's an opening.

But if you're thinking about what you're going to say, you're obviously not truly listening to what the other person is saying. It's normal to want to have an idea of what you're going to say before you say it, but it's okay to work through your response while you're giving it; enjoy the pause. As we'll explore in the essay on Power, it's low-status folks that talk the most and feel the need to fill every quiet.

Wait two seconds before answering.

Breaking in the same time a person pauses or stops talking suggests to them that you were doing the above — thinking about what you were going to say instead of genuinely listening to them. Nonverbal behaviors are more potent than verbal ones,

When someone has spoken, see if you can let your facial expression react first, suggesting that you're digesting what they've just said and giving their amazing statement the thought it deserves. Only then, after roughly two seconds, do you answer.

The sequence proceeds like this:

-They finish their sentence

-Your face absorbs

-Your face reacts

-Then, and only then, you answer

9

THE ULTIMATE CHARISMATIC GROWTH

Power

Charismatic persons are powerful people. However, this doesn't necessarily mean they're the leader of the free world or the head of a multi-national firm.

In truth, you can discover individuals who transmit Power in the humblest areas of life.

Power, simply "means being viewed as able to alter the world around us, whether through influence on or power over others, significant amounts of money, expertise, intelligence, raw physical strength, or high social status."

Powerful people can get things done, or at least they give that image.

Charismatic individuals bring people into their orbit like a magnet, and Power is the essence of that magnetic force. It's a primal attraction. Back in our prehistoric times, our survival could depend on being chummy with the big dogs at the top of the social order - those who could supply protection, food, and women. To better enable us to seek out and grab onto such people, our brains developed to cue in on body language and status signals that suggest authority.

We may have left the savanna thousands of years ago, but people are still strongly drawn to individuals who have resources, or just seem to know how to get them. Our very survival may no longer depend on our connections with such people, but our access to bigger personal and professional prospects can.

Power in the lack of Warmth and Presence is a charisma killer. A powerful man who lacks these tempering traits can be perceived as significant and impressive, but will come out as aloof, arrogant, and frigid.

How to Increase Your Charismatic Power

Increasing your charismatic Power may seem difficult; it may feel like applying for a job where you need experience to be hired, but to get that experience, you need to have that job first! Remember, though, that charisma is about how other people see you, so you don't actually have to have a 10

CHAPTER 2

million bucks or the Pope on quick dial. Nor do you need to be able to "crush your adversaries, see them driven before you, and hear the lamenting of their women" (though those things can surely help) (though those things can certainly help). In order to obtain Conan-esque power, you first only need to offer the impression that you've already had it. Fake it until you make it!

As people detect your charismatic Power and invite you into their circles of influence, you'll gain in real world power, which will make you feel and exhibit more charismatic Power - setting off a virtuous cycle that leads to more and greater success.

Offering an impression of power essentially boils down to boosting the elements humans are wired to concentrate in on when trying to discern someone's amount of it: body language and look.

Boost your confidence.

Power first begins in the head. If you feel confident and powerful, others will feel it too. Self-assurance gives you an alluring air that draws people in and makes them want to get to know you better. Developing confidence needs its own post, but for now know that the crux of confidence is mastery.

Expertise, regardless of the talent or the area of study, marks you as someone with resources, and a guy with the determination to dig to the absolute depths of a subject. Attaining mastery over something will also radically transform the way you feel about and carry yourself.

Putting the remainder of these recommendations into practice will also help enhance your confidence.

Know a little about a lot.

In addition to one area of specialization, you should also aim to know as much about as many areas as possible. Intelligence is one of the primary indicators of a man who is able to change the world around us, and the more conversations you can comfortably wade into and add into, the smarter (and more well-liked) you will look to others. How can you get a vast variety of knowledge? . Read every time you have a chance.

Become physically fit.

Your body form is one of, if not the, first thing people take in when they meet you. A fit, strong appearance sends a signal to the most primal aspects of other people's brains about your strength and ability to control and defend.

Fitness also conveys to other people that you're disciplined and capable of tolerating pain in pursuit of a goal. This is presumably why guys with an average-to-husky physique make more money than both their slender and obese friends.

Take control of your environment.

We feel most self-assured, at ease, and strong when we're familiar with our surroundings. Familiarity provides us a sense of control, which makes us feel confident. This is why groups sometimes battle over the location of negotiations before they even start negotiating. Each side wants that home-field advantage.

Speak less and slowly.

Powerful people don't just take up room physically; they also take up space in speech. Paradoxically, this doesn't mean you should be hogging the speaking time. Powerful people actually tend to speak less than low-status persons. By making their words rare, influential people raise the value of their communication. When they do talk, people listen. Harness your inner Spartan by becoming a touch less chatty and a bit more laconic with your speaking.

Powerful people also take up space in the discourse with silence. Unlike most folks, strong people aren't terrified of "awkward" silence. In fact, they relish it. They recognize that individuals will cautiously strive to fill the silence intervals. It's frequently during these episodes of frantic conversation that the other man gives up some strategic edge or vital information. This is why interrogators, job interviewers, and negotiators often resort to the silent treatment to suss out the other person's vulnerabilities.

Another approach to take up space in the conversation is to speak slowly.

Speaking rapidly shows uneasiness and anxiety. Speaking slowly displays the wisdom, thoughtfulness, and composure that powerful individuals exude.

Boost your composure.

Powerful people are composed people. They have poise, or a certain grace

and serenity about them. They don't overly nod (a sign of submissiveness), they don't fidget (a symptom of uneasiness), and they don't rely on verbal fillers like um and uh. In your next encounter with someone, act normal but focus on being as still as possible. Nod every now and then to demonstrate you're listening, but don't turn into a bobble head. Keep your hands steady and don't tap your feet.

Warmth

When you exude Warmth people regard you as being approachable, caring, and empathetic. When they're around you they feel comfortable and at ease.

Warmth meets the basic human desire to be understood, acknowledged, and taken care of — a need ingrained in our own being all the way from birth.

Warmth is your mom offering you a cup of hot cocoa when you return home from playing in the snow or combing your hair and giving you medicine as you lie unwell in bed. Warmth is your dad grabbing you into a bear hug when you show him the A+ on your test. Even if we grow up, leave the nest, and attempt to be independent, deep down we all still want to be cared for, welcomed, "at home."

Just like Power and Presence, Warmth is required for balancing the other elements and also cannot develop true magnetism on its own. A man with Power but not Warmth will come out as cold, arrogant, and aloof. A man with Warmth but not Power will be viewed as weak, eager to please, and yearning for praise.

Of all the elements of charisma, I think Warmth is the toughest to fake.

It's not too hard to convince people you're present with them (even when your mind is wandering a bit), nor to act like a guy who's got it together when you're really still working towards that objective. But people are fairly excellent at sniffing out false Warmth, and in fact have a natural instinct to positively repel when they think you're delivering the counterfeit type.

Warmth backfires when others can tell you're offering it for one reason and one reason only: to obtain something from them. Hence our disdain

for salesmen who lay the Warmth on thick for the sake of trying to close the business. It's not that you shouldn't want things from other people; pretty much the whole goal of charisma is to inspire others to do something, whether that's encouraging them to buy a product, go on a date, or serve a cause with passion. Rather, it's simply that influencing them can't be your primary motive.

For Warmth to come off as genuine it must be founded in something deeper than a strictly selfish desire. It must emerge from your own contentment with life and a deep empathy and interest for other people. A man of true Warmth enjoys getting to know persons from all walks of life; he communicates the idea that even if he doesn't acquire from them what he was seeking for, he'd still evaluate the contact to have been valuable. A man of real Warmth is one who feels that crossing paths with another individual is never a true waste.

To be truly effective in producing personal magnetism, the external behaviors that transmit Warmth to others must emerge from that most powerful but indescribable quality: a genuinely decent heart. Thus, the foundation for charismatic Warmth begins at your core.

How To Develop Warmth Within

There are two basic techniques to build your inner warmth:
Practice thankfulness. A thankful heart is a joyful heart. Studies have demonstrated again and again that individuals who practice thankfulness on a daily basis are happier and more optimistic than persons who don't.

To nurture your thankfulness, make it a routine to write down what you're grateful for every day.

As you become a more thankful guy, your capacity to put your troubles into perspective will develop, leading to a feeling of comfortable satisfaction that radiates to other people and puts them at rest.

Develop your empathy.

Empathy often called as "fellow-feeling" and that it is the most vital ingredient for a good political and social life. It's also a vital aspect in 14

CHAPTER 2

establishing charismatic Warmth. People want to be understood, and empathy is what enables us to put ourselves in their position and experience what they feel.

I'll agree that growing empathy isn't easy,here are some techniques to soften that skepticism and create deeper empathy for your fellow humans: **Consider other individuals as your brothers and sisters.**

that says we're all created by the same God, or in science that says we originated from one spot in Africa, and are even formed of the same stardust.

Either way, we're all cosmically related. Sounds a bit cliché maybe, but understanding that we're all family members undertaking the same hard trip together has frequently helped me be more empathetic when I was feeling anything but.

Interact with individuals face-to-face.

Seeing each other's facial emotions in person is what actually sparks empathy in our brains. In the absence of these indications, we're more prone to assign sinister motivations to others and experience an unrestrained hatred against them. So step out from behind your computer screen more frequently and engage with people in the real world; when you do that, the overall sensation that people are freaking' horrible that might arise from spending time online can often melt into, "Folks ain't so bad after all."

Imagine a new tale about the folks that bother you.

When you cut someone off while driving, you say to yourself, "I regret to have done that but if I don't get to this interview on time, I won't get the job." But when someone else cuts you off, you think, "What a terrible asshole." We lay our own misbehavior up to circumstances, but blame the follies of others on some underlying character deficiency. Try extending the same compassion you give yourself to others by contemplating probable explanations for why someone else could have done something impolite or disagreeable.

Be inquisitive about people.

You can't go inside another person's shoes until you actually get to know them. Ask folks clarifying questions so you can find out where they're coming from and understand what makes them tick. You may actually learn

something about life and the human condition from every single individual you meet.

The more you develop your empathy, the more you realize that everybody has hard stuff in their life that they're grappling with, and the more you'll want to become an oasis for other people – someone who lightens their burden by making them feel understood, safe, and rejuvenated even in the briefest of interactions.

Conveying Warmth To Others

So if Warmth is impossible to fake, and must be built from inside, what role do outward actions play?

First, it's possible to have a decent heart yet be poor at transmitting this generosity to others. You may not even be aware that you're coming across as distant to others, as you think of yourself as a decent man. It's crucial to not only have inner warmth, but to be able to transmit this warmth to people around you.

Second, behaving warm externally affects how warm you feel internally. It's a virtuous cycle: you behave kindly towards others, so you feel warm inside, which helps you act more warmly, and so on. In fact, behaving generously will increase your inner warmth more quickly and efficiently than reasoning your way to empathy ever would. Don't wait till you feel like an empathic person before you start behaving like it. By acting, you become. Work on both your conduct and mentality at the same time — they go hand in hand.

If you're scared about coming across as false by behaving kindly before you feel it within, don't worry. As long as you at least have a decent reason for your interactions you'll be OK. The following actions, unless you execute them clumsily or exaggeratedly, are quite simple to carry off pretty casually.

They're modest methods to just put your best foot forward with others. And 16 if they do come across as stilted the very first time you attempt them, well, don't worry about that either — you've got to start somewhere! Once you set off the virtuous charismatic Warmth cycle, it's simply a matter of time until it registers as totally real.

Think of yourself as the host.

When you bring folks over to your place, what do you do? Hopefully you seek for methods to make them feel comfortable in your house. Bring this same approach to all your encounters. When you conceive of yourself as the host in every scenario, finding out what to do to put people at ease will come more effortlessly.

Lead with a heartfelt praise.

Nothing can enhance a good relationship or break the ice in a bad one like a heartfelt praise. Sadly, we have a propensity to be fairly sparing with our friendly comments.

Put extra warmth in your voice.

Our voice expresses emotion not just via the words we say, but the tone and pitch we utilize. We transmit anger with a loud, harsh tone and we communicate friendliness and warmth with a softer, deeper tone. An simple technique to put warmth into your voice is to just smile when you talk.

Instantaneous warmth. This strategy is particularly handy for when you're chatting to someone on the phone. Without body language and facial emotions at your disposal, your voice is your sole instrument to transmit Warmth.

Mirror their body language. Research has proven that by merely copying a person's body language and style of speaking, they'll trust you and find you more appealing. Psychologists suggest that mirroring promotes limbic resonance between two people, making them more sensitive to one another.

The trick to mimicking body language is to not make it too evident. Don't mimic your discussion partner tic for tic, but if they talk quietly, reduce your own voice down a notch; if they lean back in their chair, lean back just a little too. Another strategy to make mirroring appear less visible is to let a few seconds pass before you shift into a mirrored position.

Relax your posture.

While an upright posture generates the sense of strength and confidence, it may also make you look rigid, cold, and snobbish in some settings. When you're attempting to produce Warmth, relax your posture a little. Instead of thrusting your shoulders back and pushing your chest out, allow your shoulders, back, and chest establish a natural, comfortable posture. The idea is to appear like a friendly and personable ordinary **Open up your physique.**

Besides relaxing your posture, employing "open body language" can also help you transmit Warmth to others. Instead of crossing your arms over your body, keep them at your side; instead of crossing your legs, leave them open; instead of placing a desk or podium between you and the other person, remove obstacles.

Smile, dammit.

Smiling is a simple approach to not only show Warmth to others, but also feel warm and fuzzy yourself, which assists you in communicating Warmth.

The charismatic cycle!

Studies demonstrate that smiling, even when you don't genuinely feel cheerful, will quickly make you feel happier. It's one of those times when psychology follows physiology. So to assist put oneself in a Warmth attitude, go ahead and smile.

Besides making you feel wonderful, your grin makes you more beautiful and friendly to others. Research has showed that those who smile more are viewed as more beautiful than those who don't. Psychologists and anthropologists also argue that smiling is a means for us to indicate to others that we have good intentions.

Also, as indicated before, smiling might make you sound warmer. Studies have demonstrated that people can determine who is smiling while speaking only by listening to the tone of their voice.

3

Chapter 3

How To Make Your Conversation More Charismatic **1.Be Fully Present For The Other Person.**

It can seem like being charming is all about showing off what excellent company you are, but the trick lies in lifting your partner up rather than oneself.

The paradoxical secret of charisma is that it's not about trumpeting your wonderful traits, but making the other person feel good about himself. Real charisma helps the other person feel significant; when they complete an encounter with you, they feel better about themselves than they did before. "

Back when I was a college student working at a tanning salon in between semesters, I met the Midwest's equivalent to George Clooney. This 35-year-old dream boat of a guy would come in once a week and just convert me into this jumble of joyful vibes and nice sensations every time we small spoke. He would ask me how my courses were doing, express true interest about the research I was conducting, praise my hair, and always appear really delighted to get to meet up with me. Through all of that, I didn't learn too much about him, yet I always felt he had this presence about him. Why? Because when taking all of these variables into consideration, none of the talk was about him but all of it was about me. Boom. Charisma.

2. Don't Stress If You Can't Contribute To The Conversation
A lot of us lose our confidence when we come up against a topic we can't really contribute to. But just because something is out of your profession doesn't mean you can't have fun in the chat. Instead, create room for your fear and leap in.

You shouldn't merely speak about what you know, however. You may be honest with them and demonstrate that you're inquisitive too while seeming secure. Most of us get locked up when we are caught in a debate about something we know nothing about, and suddenly, we're seeking for methods to justify ourselves instead of being comfortable with our ignorance. If you change from 'defensive mode' into 'curiosity mode', you'll look confident with the fact that you don't know about anything.

On top of that, being interested indicates that you're involved in the topic.

You could not know anything about it, but you want your conversational partner to educate you. And that's very flattering, and above all things, engaging.

3. **Ask Lots Of Questions**

If you truly want to rub someone the right way, ask plenty of questions.

Being curious and wanting to know more about a person demonstrates that you think them intriguing, which usually goes over well.

I have always found it odd that it takes a lot less expertise to ask a good question than it does to offer a decent response, but individuals who ask a lot of questions frequently end up creating the best impression.

Just think about when you're on a terrific date - how pleased are you when he or she asks for additional information about a story? It fosters a true camaraderie. To avoid end up sounding like an interviewer, use prodding questions such, "What was your favorite part of that?" or "How did you react?"

to keep the discussion moving.

4. Be Responsive With Your Body

When you sit there like a lump with your arms crossed and shoulders down like you'd rather be anywhere but there, you're not giving off the idea that 20

you're happy to be conversing with the individual. And it takes all the charm points away from you in a heartbeat. Instead, use your hands to convey that you're thrilled to be enjoying this discussion with the individual, and that you're having a good time catching up.

Using your body to accentuate and improve how you feel or what you're talking about may go a long way. Nobody believes someone who stands rigid as a board is fascinating or engaging." Use hand gestures and open up your body (i.e. don't keep your legs or arms crossed) to affirm to your friend that you're thrilled to be in this time with them and enjoying their company.

5. Bump Up Your Energy Levels

This isn't news, yet people are drawn to uplifting, joyful energy. So if you want to look charming, pump up the wattage of your passion by a bit, and others will find you all the more intriguing.

Isn't it lovely when you call someone on the phone and their voice reflects delight and excitement when they hear your name? Even if it's subtle, it makes you feel valued. A dynamic, expressive voice is one of the most powerful instruments in the world, particularly when it's resonant and sparkles with variations in pitch, speed, and volume."

Even if it's simply adding some warmth when you announce someone's name, or letting your face melt into a welcome just-for-you grin, adding a spike of excitement will go a long way in terms of charm.

6. Mirror Their Body Language

We enjoy things that seem familiar, and the more comfortable we are with a person the more we like 'em. So how can we create that degree of trust and warmth with someone we hardly know? Easy: You mimic their body language.

Research has proven that by merely copying a person's body language and style of speaking, they'll trust you and find you more appealing. Psychologists suggest that mirroring promotes limbic resonance between two people, making them more sensitive to one another. This doesn't mean you should dive into a bizarre game of Simon Says with them as you're trading anecdotes over finger snacks. Instead, keep it understated. If they talk in a slower pace,

slow your flow a touch; if they lean forward over the table, move in a little closer, too. It'll make them feel like you're on the same page.

7. Think Of Yourself As The Host

This is definitely my most favorite, life-changing piece of advice: If you want to become more charming, act like you're the host to every individual you talk to. When you invite friends or family around at your apartment, you go a little above and beyond to make them all feel welcome and snug —

and, let's be honest — little impressed. Following that principle, if you want to emit some major charm, simply go into host-mode every time you're in a discussion. That manner, making them feel welcomed will come effortlessly.

When you conceive of yourself as the host in every setting, finding out what to do to put people at ease will come more effortlessly."

So if you want to leave your wallflower, not-really-sure-what-to-do-with-your-hands days behind, simply try these modest small modifications to your conversation flow, and see what happens! Chances are, you'll be emitting your finest Marilyn Monroe charm in no time.

22

4

Chapter 4

Active listening Strategies

Listeningisoneofthemostcrucialabilitiesyoucanhave. How effectively you listen has a huge influence on your work performance and on the quality of your interactions with others.

For instance:

-We listen to get information.

-We listen to comprehend.

-We listen for delight.

-We listen to learn.

Given all the listening that we do, you would think we'd be brilliant at it!

In truth, most of us are not, and research reveals that we only recall between 25 percent and 50 percent of what we hear.

Clearly, listening is a skill that we can all benefit from learning. By being a better listener, you may boost your productivity, as well as your capacity to influence, convince and bargain. What's more, you'll prevent confrontation and misunderstandings. All of these are crucial for job success!

The approach to enhance your listening abilities is to practice "active listening." This is when you make a deliberate effort to hear not just the words 23

that another person is speaking but, more importantly, the full message being transmitted.

In order to achieve this, you must pay attention to the other person extremely attentively.

You cannot allow yourself to get distracted by whatever else may be going on around you, or by developing counterarguments while the other person is still speaking. Nor can you allow yourself to grow bored, and lose attention on what the other person is saying.

To strengthen your listening abilities, you need to let the other person know that you are listening to what they're saying.

To appreciate the relevance of this, ask yourself whether you've ever been involved in a discussion where you questioned if the other person was listening to what you were saying. You worry whether your message is getting over, or if it's even worthwhile continuing to talk. It seems like talking to a brick wall and it's something you want to avoid.

Acknowledgment may be anything as basic as a nod of the head or a simple "oh huh." You aren't necessary agreeing with the person, you are just signaling that you are listening. Using body language and other indications to indicate you are listening might also assist you to pay attention.

Try to reply to the speaker in a manner that will encourage them to continue speaking, so that you may receive the information that you need. While nodding and "oh huhing" suggests you're engaged, an occasional inquiry or remark to summarize what has been said also conveys that you are listening and absorbing his message.

Becoming an Active Listener

There are five major active listening skills you may employ to help you become a more successful listener:

1. Pay Attention

Give the speaker your entire attention, and recognize the message. Recognize that non-verbal communication also "speaks" loudly.

- Look at the speaker directly.

-Put away distracting notions.

-Don't mentally prepare a retort!

-Avoid getting distracted by surrounding forces. For example, side chats.

-"Listen" to the speaker's body language **2. Show That You're Listening**

Use your own body language and gestures to convey that you are interested.

-Nod sometimes.

-Smile and employ other facial expressions.

-Make sure that your posture is open and interested.

-Encourage the speaker to continue with tiny vocal remarks like yeah, and "oh huh."

3. Provide Feedback

Our own filters, assumptions, judgements, and beliefs might affect what we hear. As a listener, your responsibility is to grasp what is being stated. This may require you to think on what is being stated and to ask questions.

-Reflect on what has been stated by paraphrasing. "What I'm hearing is... ," and

"Sounds like you are saying... ," are effective methods to reflect back.

-Ask questions to explain particular aspects. "What do you mean when you say... ."

"Is this what you mean?"

-Summarize the speaker's statements occasionally.

4. Defer Judgment

Interrupting is a waste of time. It annoys the speaker and inhibits complete comprehension of the message.

-Allow the speaker to finish each point before asking questions.

-Don't interrupt with counterarguments.

5. Respond Appropriately

Active listening is aimed to develop respect and understanding. You are obtaining knowledge and perspective. You offer nothing by criticizing the speaker or otherwise putting her down.

25

THE ULTIMATE CHARISMATIC GROWTH

-Be frank, upfront, and honest in your answer.

-Assert your ideas politely.

-Treat the other person in a manner that you believe they would like to be treated.

How To Increase Your Charisma Through Active Listening.

What part does the capacity to listen play in charisma? What measures can you take to become a better listener?

Although it may seem like you simply need to be a good speaker to have charisma, a huge component of charisma is really being a great listener. If you take a real interest in people, they will be attracted to you.

Here are some pointers on how to create charm by increasing your listening abilities

contrary to what you may anticipate, it's considerably more vital to be a compelling listener than a charismatic speaker. If you're really interested in the other person, they'll sense it and feel connected to you.

If you want to know how to create charisma, being a thoughtful and empathic listener is vital since individuals tend to correlate the people, places, and things around them with their emotional state, even if the relationship isn't rational. This implies that how your spouse feels while talking to you is significantly more essential than what you speak about.

If you make people feel good by being really interested in them, they'll regard you as a fascinating conversationalist even if you do nothing but listen.

Tips On How To Become A Good And Emphatic Listener
Empathic Listening is a dynamic and caring process that demands for more than taking in someone else's words. You're communicating with that individual as well. You're demonstrating that you care about them, their views and emotions, and are ready to take the time to hear them out.

Listening with empathy develops rapport that maintains Care, Welfare, 26

CHAPTER 4

Safety, and Security, thriving and sets the scene for issue solutions. Knowing the individuals in your care better allows you to detect reasons of behavior and discover solutions.

I'd want to always know the appropriate thing to say in any situation to offer someone comfort and hope, to solve the issue, but I'm just human and can't comprehend and repair everything. Also, sometimes words can't repair anything.

Sometimes, letting someone know the depth of your empathy by being there, by being a sympathetic sounding board for their feelings, is all that's required at that moment. Rather of fretting about the proper words, what if we concentrated on giving our time and compassion?

7 Tips for Empathic Listening

1. Be nonjudgmental.

This isn't always easy, but letting go of your own ideas frees you to concentrate on the other person's viewpoint. Acknowledging a person's thoughts and feelings allows you to assist them. This doesn't imply you need to agree with everything the person says; it's about letting them know you care, that they matter.

2. Give the individual your entire attention.

Remove distractions. Ensure that you have the time to spend with the individual, and make sure no laptops or other gadgets are between you and them. Giving them your complete concentration indicates respect, and a person is more likely to remain calm when they feel appreciated.

3. Listen carefully(to emotions and facts) (to feelings and facts).

Soak in the words as well as the bigger vision of that person in that exact scenario. Notice tone of voice, body language, and other cues to go beyond the words and obtain insight into emotions.

4. Show that you are listening closely.

Think about your posture and nonverbal cues. Pepper in supporting

body language like eye contact, nodding, and other cues as necessary to demonstrate your concentration without interrupting

5. Don't be frightened of stillness.

Sometimes all a person needs is to be heard or know you're there. Pay attention to the context and quality of the quiet before answering. The person can be pondering about what to say next or may require a few quiet minutes to rein in emotions.

6. Restate and paraphrase.

If you speak, refer to the person's statements, ask questions, and clarify comments as required. Keep that nonjudgmental and courteous attitude, and allow the other time to answer. Remember, there's no script for Empathic Listening. Respond depending on that person, scenario, and moment.

7. Follow up.

Check with the individual to see if they have more questions or remarks.

Set up another time to meet if required.

What are methods you listen in your day-to-day life? Which tactics work best for you?

5

Chapter 5

The power of personal charisma in public Speaking.

Whenwetalkaboutcharismaandpresenceinpublicspeaking we typically think of an external force that we emit upon our audience. But the fact is that all wonderful charm originates from inside ourselves.

Developing and exhibiting this ‘personal charisma’ offers us all the building blocks we need to become a captivating speaker.

Rather than ‘inventing’ a more captivating version of ourselves for an audience, we need to disclose more of ourselves.

So how can we display our own charisma?

Learn to be authentic

1.Be comfortable with who we are

Becoming a captivating speaker needs entire sincerity. This is true of all sorts of public speaking. Good stand-up comedy, for example, requires the comic grounding what they’re saying on reality – they ‘reveal’ rather than

‘invent’ – which makes a lot more striking impression with the audience.

It also helps us relax. When we're free to be entirely ourselves in a social scenario, whether it be a home party, a business event, or a family gathering, our anxiety levels completely dissipate. We're considerably more calm and

much more confident than if we were concerned about saying the wrong thing and seeming the wrong way. The same is true of public speaking.

Authenticity also develops confidence in individuals listening to us and makes us look more charming. People trust us because they're getting to know the REAL us, and will interact all the more powerfully.

2.Overcome our own defenses

Appearing honest in front of an audience involves growing comfortable with being vulnerable.

The primary hurdle to being real is putting our guard up. We believe that we'll be criticized if we exhibit too much of our genuine selves, or that others will reject us.

In reality, the reverse is true. When we're real people sit up and take attention. They lean in to hear more from us and are more eager to interact.

So we must learn to abandon our protective barriers. People perceive inauthenticity instantly. If our face is telling one thing but our head is saying another then others will know that something isn't quite right. Don't be inauthentic to attempt to impress people. Remember; being real gives us confidence and brings people to us.

3.Discover our actual self

We're only able to develop personal charisma by feeling really worthwhile.

A feeling of personal unworthiness impedes this connection and means we feel ‘exposed’.

We look honest by exposing what’s already within us — our actual interests, beliefs and values. It’s tough to be completely sincere when we’re talking about something we don’t actually care about. Knowing about what we’re talking about and having a love for it helps give us the comfort and confidence to look real with an audience.

In order to realize our actual self we need to better understand and accept our own values and beliefs:

a) When we find ourselves vulnerable we become too preoccupied with being flawless, which holds us back. Instead we need to have an honest talk with ourselves and confess that we’re not perfect and be satisfied with that truth.

CHAPTER 5

We need to acknowledge that we lie and put forth phony versions of ourselves in certain settings. There’s no judgement involved in this, but it’s vital to notice when we do this. We need to become aware of what goes through our thoughts when we behave falsely and when we act sincerely.

Exercise – Try to think of a moment when you weren’t yourself and a time that you were honest. What do you feel in each situation? How were they different?

b) We then need to acknowledge our talents and appreciate what we give the most. This will increase our feeling of self-worth and help us to appreciate being vulnerable. Charismatic people regard vulnerability as neither unpleasant or comforting, but simply required.

Exercise - Go through and develop a list of all the good ways that you believe you affect on the world. This might be in the career, family or social life. Can we distinguish situations when we've brought out honesty in others?

By recognizing where we've benefited others this helps us strengthen our own feeling of worth.

4.Review our talents and learn to appreciate them.

Emphasise with yourself than we have worth and that we're bringing this value to our public speaking. Having this viewpoint offers us the mental fortitude against worrying about how we seem to an audience, and makes us more charismatic and present.

Playing to our strengths implies that we concentrate on what we do know rather than what we don't. We can understand that it's completely acceptable not to be flawless.

By eliminating defensiveness we lower our stress levels and become more calm. If we're shielding ourselves from probable criticism or failure then we can't be present and we'll be detached from the moment.

By leveraging authenticity and vulnerability we build the courage to be imperfect, to take chances and to be compassionate toward ourselves and others. We therefore become more charismatic.

Learn more about expressing yourself truly and convey your own story with our article on effective storytelling.

Creating an emotional contact with the audience.

Others frequently wrongly assume that charm means 'forcing' people to listen to you via sheer effort on stage. But nothing could be farther from the truth.

Rather of forcing an audience to connect with us onstage, a really compelling speaker encourages their audience to emotionally engage with what they're talking about, so 'pulling' them in. We can achieve this in a variety of ways:

1.Believe in what we're talking about Emotional involvement begins with having a profoundly personal connection with the issue we're discussing. Care about what we're talking about and the audience will care with us. Inversely, the audience will recognize when such sensations are being fabricated.

Positive thoughts towards what we're talking about will help us communicate with energy, conviction and command. It will also help us devote totally to our issue, conquering whatever emotions of vulnerability we still may have.

An audience very much loves passion and sincerity in a compelling speaker.

2.Be optimistic

An audience expects their public speaker to be upbeat and to emanate optimism. It's crucial that we come across as a friendly personality onstage.

If we're gloomy, sad or pensive then the audience will move away and the connection is gone.

3.Show empathy to your audience

The most captivating presenters mirror the beliefs, objectives and goals of the people they're talking to.

To engage with an audience we must demonstrate that we understand and sympathies with them. This may require completing research in advance, sometimes known as 'audience profiling'. We can better understand our audience in numerous ways:

Segmentation — We can examine our audience using a broad variety of variables; age, gender, geography, lifestyles, attitudes, self-perceptions and interests. This will assist us to better understand who our audience are.

Messaging - We may then structure our messaging more precisely towards

our target, employing the interests, attitudes and behaviours that best appeal to them.

Engagement - Shaping our voice in the appropriate manner, for maximum effect.

Measurement - By measuring the effect of our efforts, we may alter our public speaking to better land with people.

One method we can better understand our audience is using a 'empathy map'

An Empathy map will assist us understand our audience's wants and help us develop an emotional connection with them. Empathy maps vary in forms and sizes, but a basic empathy map has four quadrants: **Say - What the crowd says about our public speaking.**

Think - What the audience is thinking about when we're speaking. What

occupies an audience members' thoughts?

Feel - What emotions does an audience member feel about our public speaking and the event as a whole?

Do - What actions and behaviors does an audience member embody while we're speaking?

The map gives an overview of an audience member's experience and may help us better emotional interact with them.

4.Show positive body-language

Charisma stems from the physical messages we give off via our body language. We consequently aim to manage this language to wow and influence our audience. We can achieve this in a number of ways:

-Open body language with confident stance; shoulders back, head held high, feet firmly put shoulder length apart

-Controlled motions and gestures around the stage

-Warm facial expressions

-Strong eye contact with your audience

-Friendly and powerful voice; change the tone and loudness as required

-Relaxed breathing

12 attributes of a charismatic speaker

Have you ever heard a presentation and subsequently recognized how captivated you were to the presenter? No, not that type of attraction. I mean that you felt connected and uplifted while you were listening. You came away feeling happy. The speaker was so eloquent that you were impacted in some manner. Even if the presentation was about selling shoes!

That quality you encountered is called charisma. Webster defines charisma as "that extraordinary spiritual strength or personal attribute that gives an individual influence or authority over huge numbers of people." A compelling speaker creates an impact on the audience, big or little, that makes them want to come back for more. It's precisely what you want if you are attempting to sell or persuade a consumer. Charisma is not only for selling; the finest university lecturers are typically captivating speakers as well.

We connect charisma with preachers, like Billy Graham, or old-time politicians, such as Winston Churchill. Could you become a captivating speaker? The answer is yes! By breaking down charisma into its 12

component traits (given below in no particular order), you may obtain each attribute with a little time and practice: **1.Charismatic speakers are self-confident and secure. They don't look uneasy or ill at ease.**

2.Charismatic speakers appear to be enjoying themselves; they are fun, amusing, cheerful.

3.Charismatic speakers are bright & dynamic.

4.Charismatic speakers are knowledgeable about their topic.

5.Charismatic speakers look nice, they have a stage presence.

6.Charismatic people communicate without faltering, using whole sentences and good language, without "ers" and "uhs."

7.Charismatic speakers have an opinion on their topic. They care about it. You can feel their intensity, energy, and conviction.

8.Charismatic presenters tie their issue to the greater scheme of things, they are expansive, motivating, and uplifting.

9.Charismatic speakers develop a strong relationship with their

audience, they connect.

10.Charismatic speakers are optimistic in perspective, joyful, and cooperative.

11.Charismatic presenters are ordered; their ideas are clearly related and logically follow one another, with an overview at the beginning and a conclusion at the end. They are exact and comprehensive.

12.Charismatic speakers (real ones) are honest, well mannered, patient, fair, and responsible.

6

Chapter 6

The Socratic Method of Speaking

TheSocraticMethodoriginatedwiththisphrasefromthelegendary Greek thinker, Socrates: “Let us explore the matter together, my friend, and if you can dispute anything I say, do so and I will be convinced.” This ancient type of give-and-take discourse is supposedly predicated on Socrates’ view that lecturing was not an effective approach to educate all of the pupils. The Socratic Method necessitates cooperative arguing discourse between persons, asking and responding questions that inspire critical thinking, and pull out underlying presumptions.

What is the Socratic method?

The Socratic Method is a means of teaching oneself by the original sense of the term “educate.” The Latin definition of educate is “to bring out.”

Socrates identified the finest technique to promote knowledge in his pupils.

That was not by giving them things – which is termed didactic education –

but to have them say things to him, which is now called Socratic instruction.

Didactic teaching is when the speaker forces information on pupils. So, the didactic technique simply implies the learner sits and absorbs material, and 36

is supposed to learn through that process.

Socrates firmly thought that the didactic procedure did not produce any true knowledge. It, at best, pushed pupils to be excellent regurgitators of knowledge. In a didactic scenario, pupils typically recall material and regurgitate "facts", without fully knowing what they were repeating.

Since Socrates was a teacher of tremendous depth and of pretty nuanced philosophy, he required a technique to educate his pupils in a much more complete, powerful manner. What he found was that the Socratic Method –

which is simply to ask his pupils effective leading questions – would bring out of them tremendous new realizations via this questioning process.

Basically, with the Socratic Method, it is the students who are coming up with that knowledge. So excellent questions, good speaking assignments if you will, enable students to start speaking and sharing, and start coming out with startling new realizations.

This is all founded on the premise that the truth is within of you, and everything you need to know you already know, you simply just need assistance navigating and accessing that information.

How to practice the Socratic Method?

The Socratic Method is essentially about asking questions, but not just any questions. It is about asking the correct questions: questions that are thought stimulating, that delve deeper into the subject, and that motivate a higher level of thinking and sharing in order to attain a learning result that wouldn't have been achievable with typical teaching/training approaches.

The Socratic approach is typically taught to life coaches, as their main duty is not to educate coaches but to help them in uncovering the knowledge that is already within themselves. As a trainer, it is possible that you have already employed the Socratic approach in some form, even if you weren't completely aware of it. And it is actually through the Socratic method that you

have further developed your skills and knowledge as a trainer, because when participants ask questions and you have to think about and give a thoughtful answer, you are in fact benefitting from this process because it gives you the opportunity to dig deeper, to form and share your ideas in the best way possible.

Thinking about it as "the Socratic Method" is only a means of organising and comprehending the current process of asking questions and bringing forth information. There are a million various questions you may ask in any given circumstance, but here are some suggestions of questions that serve distinct goals in the training process. If you employ the Socratic approach at some portions or during the entire training, it might be beneficial to convey this to the participants so that they don't believe that your probing questions are like an interrogation and they don't feel frightened by them. Some cultures are more used to asking and being asked questions that others, so it is necessary to take this into mind as well. Body language and tone of speech come into play as well. If we think about the first question in this part, "why are you saying that", it may come across either as an invitation to share more or an accusation, depending on the way it is said and the way it is received.

I have highlighted the ones that I have found most effective in trainings, and quickly explain why.

Conceptual clarification questions

Why would you say that?

What precisely does this mean?

How does this connect to what we have been talking about?

What is the nature of…?

Can you give me an example?

This is especially beneficial for gaining a better image of what someone is saying and eliminates misunderstandings.

Probing assumptions

What else could we assume?

What else might this mean?

This one introduces a larger variety of options that may not have been explored, and opens the door to empathy and the knowledge that the same item may mean various things to different individuals.

You seem to be assuming….?

How did you pick those assumptions?

Please clarify why/how….?

How can you verify or refute that assumption?

What would happen if….?

Do you agree or disagree with….?

Probing reasoning, reasons and evidence

Why is it happening?

How do you know this?

Show me….?

Can you give me an example of that?

Helps individuals draw on their real knowledge and experience rather than merely debating ideas.

What do you believe causes…?

What is the nature of this?

Are these justifications good enough?

How can I be confident of what you are saying?

What evidence is there to back what you are saying?

Questioning opinions and perspectives

What additional ways of looking at this are there?

Helps to extend the scope of ideas and think beyond the box, might be effective especially while brainstorming.

Who gains from this?

What is the difference between….and…..?

Useful for clarifying words, for example “what is the difference between a manager and a leader?”

Why is it better than….?

What are the strengths and disadvantages of….?

How are…..and…..similar?

Can be beneficial in training linked to intercultural understanding/interreli-gious dialogue.

How could you look at this another way?

Probe implications and ramifications

Then what would happen?

What are the repercussions of such assumption?

What are the implications of….?

How does this match with what we learnt before?

Sometimes I will purposefully perform back to back sessions without debriefing, and then use these or similar questions to bring all the lessons together.

What is the best….? Why?

Why is…..important?

Questions regarding the question

What was the aim of asking the question?

Why do you believe I asked this question?

Why do you believe we completed this exercise?

Usually they (or at least one person in the group) will come up with the learning result on their own and then it may be expanded on further.

41

THE ULTIMATE CHARISMATIC GROWTH

What does it mean?

As you may have observed, all of the preceding questions are open-ended questions. Open-ended questions are questions that enable someone to offer a free-form response.

Closed-ended questions may be answered with “Yes” or “No,” or they contain a restricted selection of viable replies.

Closed-ended questions halt the discussion and eliminate surprises: What you anticipate is what you get. (Choose your favorite ice cream: vanilla, strawberry, or chocolate.) When you ask closed-ended questions, you may unwittingly restrict someone’s replies to just the things you think to be true.

Worse, closed-ended questions may prejudice individuals towards providing a specific answer. Answers that you offer may show what you are searching for, therefore individuals may be directly or indirectly impacted by the questions.

Although there is a time and place for both open-ended questions and closed-ended questions in a training, the Socratic method inherently requires open-ended questions since the purpose is to bring out more from the participants and it is the open-ended questions that may do this.

Conclude ended questions may be quite effective when you are attempting to come to a conclusion or close a process. When you are nearing the end of the session, it may be better to use a close-ended question such as “do you feel that this sufficiently summarizes what we discussed" rather than the open-ended "what other ways are there of describing this" question which can trigger a whole other line of thought that you may not have the time to continue. When selecting whether to utilize open or closed questions simply ask yourself:

Is my purpose to encourage people to open up and share more?

Or is it to easily wind up the conversation and establish some firm conclu-42

sions?

If it's the first, use open-ended questions and when appropriate (for example when you are debriefing an activity) you may add the Socratic approach. If it is the second, better stick to close-ended questions.

7

Chapter 7

Charismatic Leadership.

Everyleadershipstylehasaparticulararareaofconcentration.For instance, certain styles of leadership – such as democratic leadership

- concentrate on the growth of individuals.

Others, such as

bureaucratic leadership, concentrate on existing procedures and structures.

Today, we're going to look on a leadership style that places the attention on the leaders themselves: charismatic leadership.

What is charismatic leadership?

Charismatic leadership is described by a leader who utilizes his or her communication abilities, persuasiveness, and charisma to influence others.

Charismatic leaders, given their capacity to connect with people on a deep level, are particularly helpful inside businesses that are experiencing a crisis or are trying to go ahead.

CHAPTER 7

The traits

Every charismatic leader looks a little bit different. However, there are several fundamental features that most charismatic leaders share:

-Strong communicator

-Empathetic and relatable

-Confident

-Motivational

-Engaging and delightful

-Optimistic

You may observe that charismatic leadership has many features with transformative leadership. Whereas comparable, there's one significant difference: charismatic leaders depend on their own personality and talent to motivate their followers to action, while transformational leaders rely on a shared vision to generate change. So although most transformative leaders tend to be charismatic, not all charismatic leaders are necessarily transformational.

5 Characteristics of a Charismatic Leader When thinking about what makes a great leader in the corporate workplace, whether that be outstanding accounting, finance and information technology managers and leaders, or leaders in any field, you can't help but notice the good attributes that they possess. Typically, many leaders have similar features inside their personality that motivate their colleagues and team members to want to listen and follow their guidance.

These attributes are part of what develops a leader's charm. Most of us can identify a few leaders that we've experienced in our careers who have had an influence on us—maybe from the way they made you feel when you were in their presence to their ability to dominate a room simply by stepping into it.

Great leaders have what they call the "it" factor. Yes, it's something that comes instinctively, but it can also be learnt.

By knowing the attributes that great leaders have in common, you may strive to enhance your own charisma and become a better leader in your organization. I just came across a nice post on Entrepreneur.com that speaks about this issue. I decided to share some of the suggestions they mention as well as add a couple of my own. Take a look at the 5 Characteristics of a Charismatic Leader below.

1. Confidence

Many of the most effective and successful leaders radiate confidence. They seldom express self-doubt and are typically in control of their emotions.

To be a great leader, you will have to exercise self-confidence. You can't second guess yourself or feel bashful among your coworkers. Be careful while managing a project, to be optimistic and view the glass as half full. This can assist your confidence come over to your team and may lead to a favorable result.

2. Creativity

Charismatic leaders typically think outside the box and aren't hesitant to take chances. This implies that they tend to come up with imaginative solutions. When a difficulty develops, good leaders rise to the challenge—instead of falling to it. When they come up with unique ideas many times this may lead to positive transformation that will eventually affect the company in a beneficial manner.

3. Vision

Leaders with tremendous charisma are continually looking towards the future and ways to enhance it. They follow their objectives and know precisely what they are attempting to attain. Show that you have a vision by sharing it to people on your team. If they know you're attempting to enhance the future in any form, they will take attention.

CHAPTER 7

4. Determination

In order to realize their vision, leaders have to be determined to reach those targets. Even when they come into obstacles, they have to press through.

Show your determination as a leader by not giving up when you hit road blocks and utilize the other attributes like inventiveness and confidence to support your resolve. This will undoubtedly encourage others.

5. Communication

Great leaders are good communicators. Specifically, they know to be careful and attentive in their speech. Strong communicators do not communicate in jargon and concepts that others may or may not comprehend.

Rather, effective communicators talk in clear language that is understood by everybody. In addition, some of the finest leaders I have watched know how to utilize "stories" to get their message or point through to others. Lastly, being straightforward and polite is one of the main components I have observed lead to good communication.

How to be a charismatic leader.

Charisma and leadership should go hand-in-hand – and you may have observed that leaders without charisma struggle Leadership styles varies from one person to another but what all leaders have in common is obvious – and almost palpable – charm. However, we aren't born charismatic, it's something we cultivate along the road. It's not that tough to boost your leadership charm, however. These 10 suggestions will teach you how.

Be confident

Confidence is the most vital attribute of a competent leader. It will be exceedingly tough to inspire others if you are not confident. Lack of confidence shows that you don't trust yourself, or that you don't feel you're 47

THE ULTIMATE CHARISMATIC GROWTH

doing the correct thing.

Without confidence, leadership charisma is hard to establish. To become a more charismatic leader, you need to improve your confidence and fully trust in your talents and work ethic.

Communicate with your team

Isolation from the team or workforce is one of the most frequent leadership blunders. Charismatic leaders don't remove themselves from others; they focus on enhancing their contact with workers, customers, partners and other people. Good communication abilities excite others and develop trust.

Be creative

Good leadership charisma is all about innovative ideas. Charismatic leaders don't want to fit a set pattern; they go , and aren't scared to inspire their team to be innovative as well. Creativity is crucial because it helps us to recognize possibilities in unexpected circumstances to tackle problems ahead, and achieve great progress.

Have a clear vision

If you take a look at interviews of extremely successful individuals, especially leaders in their sectors, you will find many agree it's vital to have a clear vision. This implies you need a clearly defined objective, broken down into smaller milestones. The vision permits you to know precisely what you're doing or where you are heading.

Be mature

A forceful personality shouldn't be confused for maturity. Someone may have a forceful demeanor, yet still be mature while doing business.

CHAPTER 7

Be determined

Determination works hand-in-hand with the other secrets of leadership charm described above. To set yourself apart as a compelling leader, you need to be resolute and know precisely what you want, and how you'll get it. This is directly connected to having a clear vision.

Team members don't work properly when the leader constantly changing their opinion. Stay focused to generate charm and motivate your colleagues to work hard and follow your direction.

Be humble

We are accustomed to the concept that leaders should be confident, resolute and motivated, but they also need to be modest. Being egotistical doesn't add to charm, it takes away from it. Charismatic leaders attach a lot of importance to each employee, and listen to their issues.

Your charisma is best represented via the act of showing each employee their job is valued. Humility goes a long way and increases your leadership abilities and charm.

Self-improvement

It's acceptable to admire your work and believe in yourself but, at the same time, you should also seek to enhance current talents or acquire new ones.

Self-improvement pulls you ahead as a leader and generates charm. After all, it's totally natural; to be better, and achieve more success, you need to accept your value, and seek to grow it.

Walk the walk

The captivating leader doesn't simply 'talk the talk', they 'walk the walk'. This implies you need content and to the sort of leader that doesn't concentrate on instructing others what to do. You also need to demonstrate you accomplish precisely what you anticipate from the team. A good leader doesn't simply bully someone about; they aim to lead by example.

Set the bar high

High expectations are intimately connected to creativity. The charismatic leader encourages others to accomplish better, achieve more, and become the greatest versions of themselves they can be. This is not about creating expectations that are hard to meet, but about inspiring the team – and yourself

– to succeed.

Leadership charisma is feasible to establish or strengthen with a few actions.

Remember, it's all about believing in yourself and encouraging team members via compassion, clear vision and self-improvement.

50

Document Outline

www.ingramcontent.com/pod-product-compliance
Lightning Source LLC
LaVergne TN
LVHW050345160826
845677LV00014B/3800